THE ABSOLUTELY WORST FART BOOK

Written By:
Herbert Kavet

Illustrated By:
Martin Riskin

© 1992
by **Ivory Tower Publishing Company, Inc.**
All Rights Reserved

Manufactured in the United States of America

30 29 28 27 26 25 24 23 22 21 20 19 18 17 16 15 14 13 12 11 10 9 8 7 6

Ivory Tower Publishing Co., Inc.
125 Walnut St., Watertown, MA 02172
Telephone #: (617) 923-1111   Fax #: (617) 923-8839

INTRODUCTION

Why another Fart Book? The three we've already published have sold over three million copies. Enough is enough. Surely there are some other subjects, even other bodily functions, to burden the English speaking public with. There are, on the other hand, evidently enormous numbers of farters out there farting endless wet and dry, silent and noisy, smelly and inane farts. So many categories, so many classifications and no government funding to codify them. It may not be a fun job, but somebody's got to do it.

There are "Your Farts" and "My Farts". Mine are rather pleasing and never smell offensively while yours range from horrendous to life threatening.

My farts are satisfying	Your farts are disgusting
Mine are newsworthy	Yours are annoying
My farts are dignified	Yours are noisy
Mine are aromatic	Yours are smelly
My farts are original	Yours are rude
Mine are imaginative	Yours are in poor taste

THE CLASSIFICATION OF FARTS

THE COPY MACHINE FART

It's one thing to fart around a stranger and quite another to fart in the presence of a co-worker with whom you must spend every day. The Copy Machine Fart is an office fart and is among the most embarrassing sort. A clever farter will, of course, try to blame the machine by jiggling a button and mumbling something about ozone or toner. You probably won't fool anyone. Our copier goes on the blink about once a week and I wonder if it's this fart that clogs up its delicate insides.

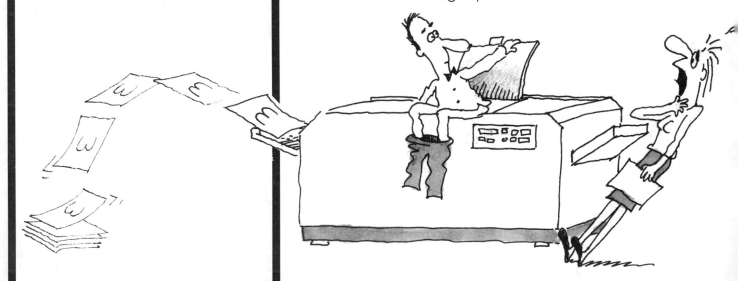

No one has ever heard this fart. It may cloud the room in brown fog or cause canaries to drop out of the sky, but any piano player worth his fortissimo will improvise a little arpeggio at the appropriate moment to mask the sound. Artists are such a clever bunch.

THE PIANO PLAYER'S FART

THE
SIT-UP
FART

Everyone who has ever done a sit-up knows this fart. It's almost totally involuntary and issues forth with a rather healthy sounding blast of air. It's downright hell, of course, on the poor fellow holding your feet at the moment.

It doesn't matter if coffee or oatmeal or two pounds of bran is the trigger, the Breakfast Fart is a satisfying part of everyone's morning routine. Better in the privacy of your own house than, say, in a car pool, I've always felt, and the presence of a full size newspaper is convenient for wafting the fumes about.

THE BREAKFAST FART

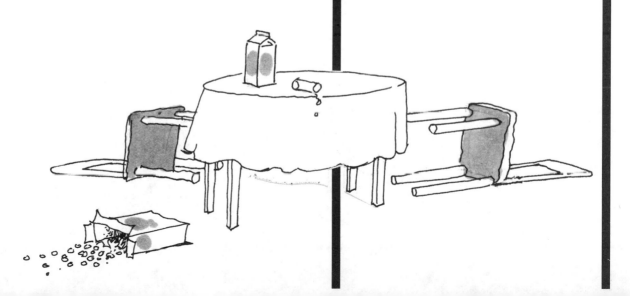

THE AIRLINE FART

The thick foam seat cushions (suitable as a flotation device in the unlikely event of a water landing) stifles this fart; kind of just gobbles it up. But, after all you are on a plane and you have to leave sometime and when you do you set free all the farts you kept the lid on (so to speak) during the flight. You will notice that the flight attendants are clever enough to avoid these lingering odors by rushing to the door as soon as the plane lands.

Beautiful girls don't fart. No way. They don't fart even after eating broccoli or spending a night drinking beer and nothing you can say can change my mind about this. Really beautiful girls can't even spell F-A-R-T.

THE BEAUTIFUL GIRL FART

THE DEAR GOD DON'T LET ME FART NOW FART

It's no place to fart and there's no place to hide and there's no one to blame. With this fart you just tighten your muscles and pray it will go away. The situation is usually so embarrassing with The Dear God Fart that most people would rather explode than fart.

Way out in the woods there's no one to hear and no one to offend. No one but you even knows it exists. The fart itself might knock squirrels out of the trees, but the solitude of the place gives it a satisfying and somewhat mysterious air. If you're hunting you can kiss away any game that may be downwind.

THE OUT IN THE WOODS ALONE FART

THE OLD MAN FART

Two old codgers were sitting on a park bench. One leaned a bit to the side and farted a silent, typical old man's fart. The other, whose sense of smell was still pretty good, asked him a bit sharply, "Did you just fart?" "Of course," the farter indignantly replied, "You don't think I always smell like this, do you?"

Fancy toilets in hotels and restaurants have this attendant who hangs around all day and hands you a towel and brushes your jacket and then expects you to tip him in this dish with quarters and dollars in it. It's more embarrassing in Europe where the attendant is usually a woman.

Well, farting, even in the privacy of an attended restroom marble cubicle, flusters me 'cause I always feel this attendant is listening, maybe even rating you. It leads to a stifled whiny fart that is a pity in such opulent surroundings.

THE ATTENDED RESTROOM FART

THE MORNING BATHROOM FART

This is an all alone fart. It's acceptable in even the best society and is one of the most satisfying I know. This fart may fill the room with haze and crack the plaster on the walls but no one can deny you this booming, welcome to the world, wake up extravaganza.

Being a highly educated member of the medical profession, you'd think a doctor fart would be a pedigreed fart with a more prophylactic composition. No way. Doctors fart noisy and silent and smelly farts just like you and me but they make them seem somehow more acceptable by calling them things like "flatulence", or "passing gas", or "intestinal pressure". These are all just regular farts so don't be fooled.

THE DOCTOR FART

THE NURSE FART

Nurses are some of most regular, natural, salt of the earth people you can imagine. They don't fart white farts or anything like that, and seldom take advantage of their ability to blame any really embarrassing farts on their patients. Nurses, fortunately, don't find body functions like this particularly interesting and I doubt any nurse has ever bought a fart book.

This isn't a fart blown by a doctor but a fart you can't restrain while waiting for the doctor in the little examining room. You spend lots of time waiting in these little rooms because doctors are real busy people and they don't want to have to wait for you while you're taking off your underwear or anything. If you forget to take along a magazine, there's nothing much to do in these little rooms so I suppose it's as good a place as any to fart. When the doctor does come in, however, he or she will know you did it. There's no escaping that. Then again, maybe that's part of the exam.

THE DOCTOR EXAM ROOM FART

THE DIVER'S FART

Scuba divers and other people who play in the water wear neoprene suits to keep them warm. There is a terrible secret to these suits concerning peeing in them to warm you up when the water is really chilly, but that's not a subject for this book. Farts can offer the same warmth plus a little extra buoyancy which is always appreciated in the water.

The rubber suits do act as a fart preservative and the full aroma will whoosh out when you take the suit off. If you find this embarrassing, you can lift an edge with a finger and let the fart bubble away while you're still underwater.

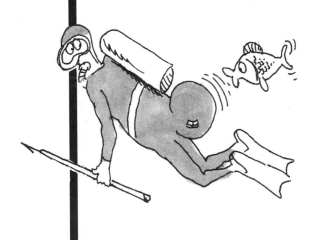

This fart used to be my favorite when I was single and did all my marketing alone. You fart in an empty aisle and then whip your cart around a corner to escape. The fart kind of hangs there quietly occupying space until someone else comes along.

The next shopper innocently rolling down the aisle is met by the mystifying odor which they can't quite be sure isn't coming from a food package. More shoppers cut their marketing trips short because of this fart than for any other reason.

THE SUPERMARKET FART

THE CLASSROOM **FART**

I did this fart once in the 2nd grade. It was a loud, sharp, totally unexpected report that dissolved the class into laughter. Mrs. Leprechaun didn't think it was so funny and angrily asked if I had to use the "lavatory". I shook my head no, not being absolutely certain what a lavatory was, and just tried to disappear into my desk.

They put out all these raw vegetables, broccoli and carrots and stuff so you won't feel too guilty eating the salted nuts, baked brie, and other life threatening snacks later on. These raw vegetables cause some people to fart but it's tough as hell to identify the farter because the room is crowded and everyone is moving around. If you see someone jumping from one group to another, that person is probably the mystery Cocktail Party Farter.

THE COCKTAIL PARTY FART

THE PIANO MOVERS' FART

You don't want to be around when this fart isfarted. It's not that I have anything against piano movers but these fellows are big strong hulks of muscular flesh and their farts are proportionately robust. A piano mover who has had a beer or two with a lunch of franks and beans is a gentleman who should be given his own space for the afternoon. You'll know when he farts.

These farts could be by the barber or hairdresser but the ones I'm talking about are by the customer. The sheet or cloth that covers you keeps the fart contained until the person cutting your hair takes it off. Then all at once all the farts you farted during the haircut escape. I used to think the barber snapped the sheet to clean off the little hairs that get stuck on it but now I suspect that motion is to clean the air for the next customer.

THE BARBER SHOP FART

THE POP FART

This fart is identified primarily by its sound which is a clean popping sound like a cork in a bottle of French champagne. You will know immediately when you've executed a Pop Fart because people near you will raise their hands almost involuntarily as if expecting a little champagne toast.

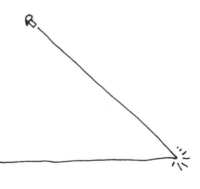

This can be a fart by the animal, of course, and if you've spent any time at Busch Gardens or your local zoo you know just how big this fart can be. But the fart I'm referring to is the Elephant Fart that some poor human being farts. This fart is so powerful that the farter feels like his (this is mainly a male fart) very bowels are generating a vacuum that the food from his stomach rushes to fill as the fart leaves his body. People get really hungry after an Elephant Fart.

THE ELEPHANT FART

THE SAILOR FART

There is absolutely no truth to the oft repeated fairy tale that prolific farters can make a sailboat go faster. Even the most fanatical racers discount this means of propulsion. A Sailor Fart is simply a fart by a sailor and knowing what these guys drink, you'd better hope to be standing to windward whenever one is released.

This fart always seems much louder than it really is. Librarians are such quiet people that when they have a little gas problem it's almost a matter for the board of directors. Librarians can describe a fart much better than the rest of us 'cause they have a surplus of words available. Doesn't "crepitation" sound much more dignified than "blowing a big one"?

THE LIBRARIAN FART

THE CINEMA FART

When you fart in a movie theater you hope the fart will rise straight up and be purified somehow by the air conditioning system before it can offend anyone. This is rarely the case. Everyone smells the smell and realizes the terrible gaffe that someone has committed, but the darkness makes positive identification chancy. By the time the lights go on and the coats come off the laps, no one can fix the exact location of anything and the farter escapes in the shuffling crowd. Popcorn, incidentally, makes many people fart and you wonder how the snack became so popular in the close confines of a movie theater.

You've traveled all week, rushed to breakfast, eaten rich foods, stayed up late, lacked privacy, perhaps were repelled by out-houses or squeezed in airline toilets. But, now you're home and comfy in the familiar seclusion of your own toilet with your own magazines and what better place to fart the fart that has been building the whole time you were away. As satisfying as sex to some people.

THE FINALLY HOME IN YOUR OWN BATHROOM FART

THE
DISAPPOINTMENT
FART

This is a fart that is a disappointment because the farter had some more serious business in mind when the fart was farted. It's probably best explained by that most famous of all restroom graffiti:

Here I sit so broken hearted
Came to shit but only farted

When I was a kid, the last line read "paid a dime but only farted" which seemed much sadder. But they did something to all those pay toilets and you don't seem to see them anymore.

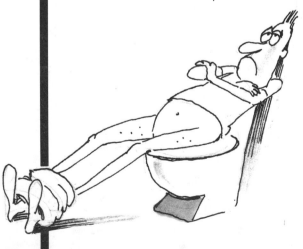

There are many bars where a well-tuned thunderlike fart is a positive sign of virility. In these places a booming fart may be applauded and the farter even stood a beer or two. Women are treated with great respect in these bars but they certainly are not expected to fart.

THE BAR FART

THE SKIER'S FART

This is a quiet fart that is muffled in many layers of polypropylene and wool and is virtually undetectable in the great outdoors. Skiers swaddled in down parkas with face masks and goggles will never even notice another skier's fart. This is all well and good considering how icy, black diamond trails produce a nervous stomach in so many people.

This is the kind of fart when your doctor tells you they'd like to run some tests and to bring in a urine specimen, a semen sample, and a stool smear, and your wife says, "That's easy. Just give them a pair of your underpants." It's that kind of fart.

THE LAB TEST FART

THE VERY DRY FART

This fart is so dry, it's like farting talcum powder. It's an odorless, fine fart like an expensive, aged wine and its lack of moisture makes it almost painful when it puffs out. The Very Dry Fart is frequently a senior citizen fart that is common with people who retire to Arizona or New Mexico.

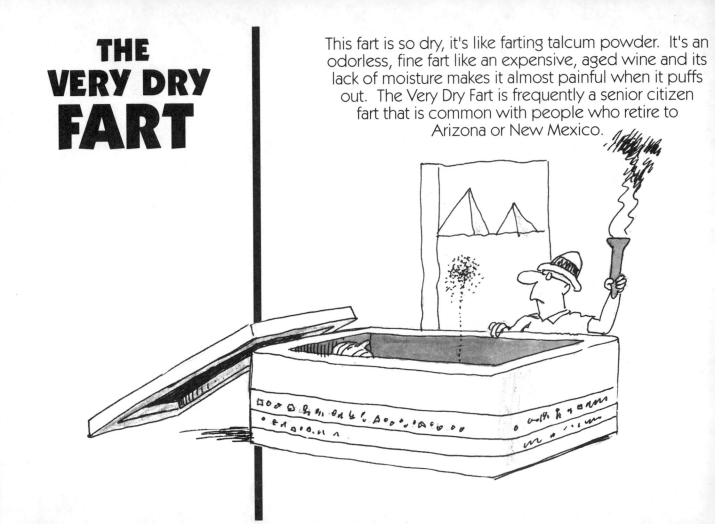

THE MISTAKEN FART

The Mistaken Fart isn't a fart at all. It's a noise. It's the squeak of a rubber shoe, or vinyl cushion meeting a wet bathing suit, or air squeezed out of a rubber duck. People who hear this fart assume it is real and react with a glare, avoidance, applause or whatever. The fun part with this fart is watching the person who made the noise try to repeat it again and again to prove he didn't fart.

BROIKK!

THE OH MY GOD FART

This is not a pleasant fart to write about. Let's see now how I can put this delicately because if nothing else this is a delicate, tasteful book. The Oh My God Fart is when you fart and a little more than gas escapes that powerful sphincter muscle. It's also referred to in some places as the "Change Your Underwear Fart."

You hug a loved one and the exuberance of the squeeze seems to press out a little blip. With someone you're very close to, you can just laugh it off, but it's mighty embarrassing with strangers. Then again, you probably shouldn't be going around hugging strangers anyway.

THE HUG FART

THE REDNECK FART

This fart is when a bunch of good ol' boys are leaning on a pickup truck "tawkin' about huntin' " and downing a few sixes of some of that good imported stuff that comes from Milwaukee. The Redneck Fart is only done outdoors 'cause the rumor is, this blockbuster leaves few survivors in closed quarters.

It's not truly the fart that lifts the cheek, but rather the person who kind of tilts to one side or the other to slip out a fart without having it make a fizzy noise. The Cheek Lifter Fart is a dead give away as to the identity of the farter. My wife has gotten so good at recognizing this fart that I swear she can detect a tilt no thicker than the page this is written on.

THE CHEEK LIFTER FART

THE JAPANESE FART

This fart is a polite, quiet fart with sort of a FLEEST sound. Some people think it has a fishy odor but the fart can be farted by Hungarians or Cubans or anyone, not only Japanese so I think that's just a stereotyped opinion. Most Japanese, however, fart this one when they're doing one of those little bows. Like I said, it's a polite fart.

CLICK!

This is a very difficult fart to detect. The farter has had 40 years to perfect his or her farting technique and is usually a master of concealment. A 40-year-old is still young enough to be original and artful, yet sufficiently mature to be cunning and crafty. Slammed doors, quick exits, opened windows, striking matches, rattled newspapers - hell, I use them all.

THE OVER 40 FART

MASTER FARTER

THE PICKLED HOT PEPPERS FART

I have a friend who brought me some homemade really hot pickled peppers. Those devils thundered through my intestinal tract like a bunch of cave men carrying home fire from a volcano. This has to be the hottest fart known to man. If you fart this fart while sitting on dry grass or straw, you're liable to burn yourself to death.

This fart can be farted by carpenters or by other people who are the kind that usually smash their fingers with hammers. The fart is characterized by the BANG BANG sound it makes. The report is so loud that the farter gives an involuntary jerk and if he (women never do this fart) keeps it up, he will invariably get a terrible headache. Not a fun fart.

THE CARPENTERS' FART

THE WEIGHTLIFTERS' FART

You get this big guy straining and pulling to push out a few more reps. Suddenly, without warning, BAPHOOT! This enormous explosion erupts and shocks the lifter who isn't really sure if he's farted or split his shorts. The other guys in the gym aren't so sure either but will generally avoid the area in question.

This fart is very common among Jews during the 8-day holiday of Passover. At this time, Jews eat Matzoh instead of bread. The sudden change from nice soft bread to the hard yeast-free Matzoh plays havoc with almost everyone's digestive system. The Matzoh Fart is an extremely dry fart, even drier than the Dry Fart. Some people swear they are farting Matzoh crumbs.

THE MATZOH FART

THE TAXI FART

A Taxi Fart is a particularly rank and unpleasant fart. It's a fact that more people fart in taxis than in any other kind of vehicle. Taxi drivers themselves are among the worst farters in the human race. Many big-city police departments have the cab companies put in these bulletproof partitions to protect the passengers from the drivers' farts. Each year thousands of lives are saved by them.

This is a super, ego-building fart. Loud and resonant as it bounces off the tile walls of the shower, it amplifies itself and sounds much more magnificent than it truthfully is. The fart is totally odorless as the water carries it away. One of my favorites.

THE SHOWER FART

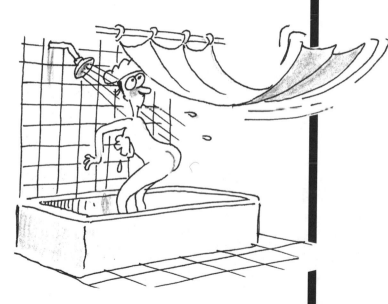

THE TEDDY BEAR FART

No, teddy bears don't really fart. This is a fart that is done in the presence of a teddy bear. It cannot be an offensive fart since the teddy bear loves you and understands you and knows you love it too. A Teddy Bear Fart is kind of fluffy and pleasantly fragrant. It's mostly a ladies fart.

Ooooh ooooh oo goes the Trombone Fart, just like the sound of the instrument. Except since there usually is no band around, everyone will look at you and sort of expect a parade. Hardly any fart surprises people more. Once they realize there is no parade everyone goes away disappointed.

THE TROMBONE FART

THE CAMPER FART

Blame them on the day's hard exertion, the freeze dried dinners or the air mattress that bounces you around. Swear to your camping buddies that they kill mosquitoes and keep bears away. It doesn't matter because this genuinely awful fart is a curse in the close proximity of a tent. Every camper knows it and dreads it and wise campers choose their tent mates very, very carefully.

This is a little fart. Perhaps even a teeney weenie fart. The name comes from its feel, which is perfectly round as it escapes from your much bigger behind. This cute diminutive fellow rolls its way smoothly and agreeably into the big world like an oil covered marble, bringing momentary pleasure to its farter and only a minimum of discomfort to passersby.

THE ROUND **FART**

THE FOOTBALL FART

A Sunday or Monday night fart brought on by beer and crisp salty snacks. It's strictly a male fart, robust and full flavored as it reverberates off the T.V. screen and an enthusiastic farter will often time it to coincide with a touchdown cheer.

Ouch. If there can be a totally uncomfortable fart, this is it. The name comes from its feel which is like a nylon bristle bottle brush being pulled through your backside. "Fhizzist" it goes and you're left with a stinging sensation and a rear that seems to have been brushed clean.

THE FIZZY FART

THE JERSEY FART

This is strictly a response fart. When you tell someone you're from "Joisey" and they ask, "Which exit, ha ha ha." You answer with, "BLATT". The Jersey Fart. That sure fixes them and really lets them know where you're from.

This is a very private and beautiful fart and I would not have been so uncouth as to include it in this silly book but it's not so easy coming up with all these farts. An author has desperate moments when he feels it's necessary to draw upon even the most intimate fart to fill in a few more pages. To put it most delicately, the Lovers' Fart is a fart that slips out of a man or woman at the point of orgasm. It just sort of escapes along with everything else that escapes at that moment, and no one even notices, what with the screaming and everything feeling so good.

THE LOVERS' FART

THE MARVIN SCHECTOR FART

Marvin lived in Brooklyn, I think, and was a fat, oily kid who bullied me one summer at Camp Lokanda. Marvin was very proud of his farts - crude, mouthy sorts that he would amplify at night by lifting the blanket on his cot. Marvin, if you read this, give me a call 'cause I'm bigger than you now and I'd like to push your face in.

This is a very expensive fart. Big city lawyers bill their time in the $250 per hour range. They divide their hours into tenths or quarters depending on some secret formula that enables them to maximize their client's bills. When a lawyer stops to fart on your time, you're billed for it the same as phone calls, thinking, nose picking, or whatever else the lawyer does while working on your problem. One fine old Boston firm breaks out the partner farts separately and bills them at a standard rate of $65 each.

THE LAWYER'S FART

THE DOOR FART

Oh, this is a clever fart. The farter carefully times this fart whether coming or going to leave it inside or out. If the farter is possessed of naturally quick instincts, he or she can even time the slam of the door to cover any embarrassing noises. The Door Fart is one of the most useful farts and it is put into service much more than you'd ever imagine.

This is a distinctly different fart from the Door Fart and actually a close cousin to the Elevator Fart. It is a dastardly fart that is left in a quarter of a revolving door. The fart goes round and round, invisibly surprising each new person passing through the door as it momentarily traps them in its aroma. Only nasty people fart the Revolving Door Fart.

THE REVOLVING DOOR FART

THE ORDINARY FART

Common as mosquitoes on a mid-summer Michigan lake, the Ordinary Fart is, well, ordinary. It hardly gets noticed by close family members; its single moderated poof just sort of slips or pops out without much ado and goes on its merry way.

Any fart where the farter is reading a newspaper can be referred to as a Newspaper Fart. Experienced farters know the newspaper can be used to waft the fart a little away or the pages can be rustled to screen moderate noises. They are more sophisticated about these things in Europe and some newspapers, like *The London Financial Times*, are even tinted in a tan color.

THE NEWSPAPER FART

THE
THING-A-MA-JIG
FART

This is more a feeling fart than a hearing fart. It's identified by something that feels like a "thing-a-ma-jig" which until that moment the farter never realized resided up his "you know where". When the poor farter farts this fart, the full size and shape of this "thing" becomes evident and as it comes out in a rush, the farter is first horrified and then gratefully relieved. Very rare.

"Pooht, pooht, pooht, pooht" goes this evenly spaced noisy fart you can almost visualize mowing down hordes of charging communists. It works, of course. There are hardly any communists left these days, are there?

THE MACHINE GUN FART

THE FIASCO FART

This fart is quite similar to the Disappointment Fart and in fact many people mistakenly think it's the same thing. The farting cognoscente, however, understands that the Disappointment Fart refers to a fart that appeared in place of a bowel movement while the Fiasco Fart is a fart that totally devastates the person after specific intestinal planning and doctoring.
Perhaps it's best explained by the biblical expression:

"Everything cometh to him who waiteth provided he who waiteth dranketh prune juice last night."

You know this fart because at one time or another everyone meets it. You feel it inside but the moment is inappropriate to let it out. Then when a quiet opportunity arrives to allow it to escape, it is nowhere in sight. Here you have this prisoner in your large intestine clambering to be let free and when the time is ready, the little ingrate disappears. It leaves you with an uneasy feeling because you know the fart has to be lurking somewhere but you can't quite put your finger on where.

THE DISAPPEARING FART

THE OZONE LAYER FART

This is a very big fart, a gargantuan fart. A fart big enough to blow holes in the ozone layer. Anyone who has ever experienced an Ozone Layer Fart will seek outdoor employment for the rest of his or her life and will never keep any pets like canaries that have delicate respiratory systems.

This fart is quite common 2-24 hours after eating Chinese food. It probably has something to do with the monosodium glutamate or bean sprouts or whatever. The fart has a singular high-pitched tone which manages to reach an even higher note just at the end. Then when you think the fart is totally over, a short, even higher tone sounds forth and you feel hungry again.

THE CHINESE FOOD FART

WOO HU BING
CANTONESE
SZECHUAN
CUISINE

THE SATISFACTION FART

This is an alone fart. Its passage is smooth and satisfying and no one is around to disturb your equilibrium. The Satisfaction Fart leaves the farter with a contented glow of well being and a feeling that all is right with the world. This fart feels so good, it makes you think of starting a business that will allow you to stay in a bathroom all day.

This is a fart done in the presence of a group of good friends. The one about to fart yells, "Hold your breath" and everyone does, and then the person farts. It's supposed to protect your friends from horrible smells but most people have to breathe eventually so it seems to me the relief is at best temporary.

THE HOLD YOUR BREATH FART

THE ASPARAGUS FART

Everyone knows how asparagus gives a wonderful aromatic essence to your pee. Some people claim this same fragrance in their farts after eating asparagus. I, for one, can say hogwash. I've never experienced that kind of bouquet in my farts and my farts have as delightful a pungence as any I know. People who claim asparagus makes the fart fragrant, are the same kind of people who think their doody doesn't smell.

Phift, phift, phift it goes, never less than three little toots. A dry soft pleasant fart that is never offensive and always brings memories of cookouts on fine summer days. The Corn on the Cob Fart is one of the main reasons the Jolly Green Giant always seems so jolly.

THE CORN ON THE COB FART

THE INDIAN FART

A stealthy fart that creeps up on you silently, when you don't expect it, then rushes out with a roar and a whoop. The Indian Fart relies on surprise and stupefying speed to achieve its effect. Often brought on by experiments with fire water, this fart always stuns the farter and everyone within its range.

Blip, Blip, Blip goes the Goldfish Fart. This soft beauty is a women's and children's fart. Its delicate, low volume pressure seldom offends or alarms people. It's nice to write about a gentle fart, for a change, that regularly brings a little surprised smile to the face of the farter. If there are any goldfish in the room, they will kiss the side of their bowl.

THE GOLDFISH FART

THE CROTCHLESS PANTY FART

I think when people buy crotchless panties, farting is not what they have in mind. Crotchless panties are for romantic sexual pursuits, not humble body functions. People (mostly women) who wear these sexy things, and I wish I knew more of them, say they give farting an entirely different feel, sort of naked and very sensuous.

It's been a struggle all evening as your bowels grumble and you strain to contain the lurking monster within. But, now it's time to depart and relief is just a moment away. Some people lose it here and fart just at the door - others hang on a moment more and maybe make it outside. Either way the smart farter just says "Good-bye" and doesn't look back.

THE GOOD-BYE FART

THE FIRST DATE **FART**

This is probably the most embarrassing fart of them all. Here you are, on a Saturday night, trying to make a swell impression on this girl or guy when an unwanted fart comes along to show your date just what a clod you really are. How mortifying.

Some innocent person comes into the room where a fart has just been farted. Maybe they want to sit down and talk or watch a little TV or just walk through the room. But then they smell the fart and say "Whew" and leave as quickly as possible. Common as dirt.

THE WHEW FART

THE QUEUE FART

Queue is a British word for waiting in line. I was going to call this the "Waiting in Line Fart", but thought Queue sounded lots classier. Anyhow, you're waiting in line and someone farts and it's really embarrassing and everyone sort of scrunches away from the farter so a big gap opens up. You hope the line will move faster so you can get away from the smell but usually it doesn't.

This is a new fart. It's a homosexual fart and it involves a condom that sort of got lost along the way. I don't know many homosexuals and I don't know much about what they do or about this condom fart but I hear that it makes a really funny sound and everyone laughs a lot. Maybe that's where the term "Gay" comes from.

THE CONDOM FART

THE LABORATORY FART

Here you have all these people standing around doing experiments in this antiseptic atmosphere with white coats and maybe even masks over their noses and mouths and purified water and everything and someone farts. You can imagine the effect and it's called the Laboratory Fart.

It's a fact that most product recalls and unfavorable medical side effects are due to the presence of farters in laboratories. The federal government has issued grants to researchers trying to evolve scientists who don't fart.

Farmers fart like real people who work in offices and factories, except farmers have all these animals around who pretty much smell like farts anyway, so no one knew about it until 1942. Around that time, with so many men off to war, farmers started going to square dances and someone noticed, "Hey, these farmers are farting just like everyone else" and that's how The Farmer Fart was discovered.

THE FARMER FART

THE MOTHER-IN-LAW FART

This fart was described to me by a CPA named Thomas who lives in New York. The fart is in the bursting category, loud and short-lived, but often a repeater, the same sound being emitted in quick succession several times. Thomas' mother-in-law, Bernadine (that's really her name) is an ample woman who, for comfort, frequently dresses in sweat suits. She particularly enjoys sending this fart in Thomas' direction during family functions while maintaining a totally composed outward appearance.

This is such a bad fart that even atheists say a silent prayer when they fart it, thanking God they are alone. If they are not alone, of course, the fart immediately becomes an "Oh My God Fart" as the farter realizes he or she has gone too far this time. Many people have been drawn back to their religious roots by the presence of this most horrible fart.

THE SILENT PRAYER FART

THE FOREIGN FART

You know how when you used to go into someone's house of a different ethnic, racial, or religious background, the house, especially the kitchen, would smell funny? The foods being cooked were different. Before the days of Thai, Indian, soul, and Northern Italian restaurants on every corner, those foreign food smells were unknown to most people and they were strange.

It's the same with foreign farts. They, well, have a unique odor and sound weird to us. The world may be shrinking but if you see a fuzzy foreigner turn a little red and gently lift a cheek, you'll probably be a lot happier evacuating the area.

This fart is low in tone and varying in pitch so it resembles someone mumbling. People will turn to the farter and say, "What did you say?" The farter is usually mortified and turns red in the face which is when everyone knows it was a Mumble Fart. If the Mumble Fart farter was at all clever, he or she could answer, "Oh, particularly nasty weather," or something like that and probably get away with the whole thing.

THE MUMBLE FART

THE SEPTUAGENARIAN FART

By the time someone reaches 70 years of age (that's what a Septuagenarian is, you dummy, not someone with a birthday in September) their plumbing may not be working as well as when they were younger. That's why you see all those ads for laxatives, diuretics, antacids, suppositories and such around retirement areas. Well, when Septuagenarians fart, they fart out all these chemicals and they have to be careful not to stand near an open flame or they just might cause a fire.

The head of production at Ivory Tower Publishing brought this fart to my attention. He eats garlic bagels for breakfast each day. This fart doesn't really smell like garlic though; in fact, very few people have ever gotten close enough to smell a garlic fart, garlic breath being what it is. Garlic on your breath, of course, keeps vampires away and it's possible the Garlic Fart also keeps vampires away 'cause I haven't seen any around our office since this fellow started working here.

THE GARLIC FART

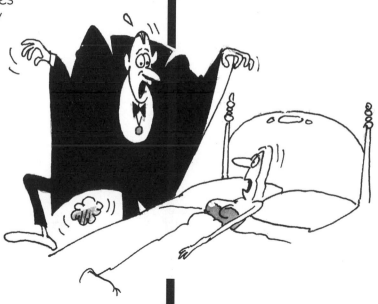

THE FANNY BURP

People need cute, inoffensive words for kids to use to describe farts. You don't want little toddlers running around using foul words, do you? I suppose Fanny Burp is as good an inoffensive term for a kiddy fart as any. In my family, we called farting "shooting marbles" which is as ridiculous as you can get. All these terms work fine until the kid goes to school. Early in his or her first week, some wise ass kid will say, "Hey, that's not a Fanny Burp, it's a FART". And your baby's innocence will start to vanish from that moment.

Some misguided people think their farts smell like flowers. These very important people also go through the express lane at a supermarket with a full load of groceries, carry two suitcases onto a plane, and probably park in handicapped spaces. There is NO SUCH THING AS A FLOWER FART not even by investment bankers who have been Republicans all their life.

THE FLOWER FART

THE CANADIAN FART

This is a friendly little fart, with no great pretensions, that sounds a little like, "EH, EH, EH," when it comes out. Sometimes it is a repeater and you'll want to turn around and answer the person, but that's ridiculous 'cause it's sort of like talking to an asshole.

There really is no such thing as a Septic System Fart. As far as I am concerned, it's a PLOY, not a fart. A bold farter will try to hide a fart by sniffing the air and announcing, "Hey, the septic system is bubbling up again." Only one person has ever been fooled by this ploy and he was only six.

THE SEPTIC SYSTEM FART

THE TOUCH TONE FART

"Beep boop beep beep boop beep beep." Oh yes you say, the Touch Tone Fart. One fellow from Milwaukee got so good at this fart that he could telephone his mother in St. Louis without putting any coins in a pay phone. The next thing you know, someone will be using farts to break into the Pentagon's secret computer system.

The phone company specifically calls for seven tones on a call because so few Touch Tone Farters can fart that many times.

BEEP BEEP BEEP BEEP BEEP BEEP

Based on black bread, greasy sausage, and vodka, the Russian Fart is perhaps the most frightening of all foreign farts. Russian men and women alike will cut loose with such a fart that the force and shock will throw you into doubt about the wisdom of any cultural exchange with these people. After experiencing this fart, you'll understand why the Soviet Union broke apart.

THE RUSSIAN FART

THE COMMUTER FART

This fart is also often called the Car Pool Fart. There you are, first thing in the morning, the coffee is just starting to work and you're stuck in slow-moving traffic with no relief until you reach the office. You really hate to do this to your car-pool buddies.

Most people try to slip out a couple of small ones hoping they'll be muffled by the seat cushion. One scheme I always use is to roll down the window "to check the weather."

What makes The Absolutely Worst Fart? I doubt it is odor or loudness alone. I suspect the worst fart is the one done in the most embarrassing circumstances. I always thought the "First Date Fart" had potential as the worst, though others tell me about farts at weddings, job interviews, in saunas and other unthinkable locations.

I'd like to invite all you creative readers to send in your "Absolutely Worst Farts". I'll see if I can put them together into another "Worst Fart Book". While I can't return or acknowledge any but the greatest submission, I will send a free copy of the book if we use yours.

THE ABSOLUTELY WORST FART

You may send directly to us for the books below. Postage is $1.50 for the first book and $0.50 for each additional book.

TRADE PAPERBACK BOOKS $5.95

2400 N Sex On Your Birthday
2402 N Confessions From Bathroom
2403 N Good Bonking Guide
2404 N Sex Slave
2405 N Mid-Life Sex
2406 N World's Sex Records
2407 N 40 Happens
2408 N 30: The Big Three-Oh
2409 N 50 Happens
2411 N Geriatric Sex Guide
2412 N Golf Shots
2415 N Birthdays Happen
2416 N Absolutely Worst Fart
2417 N Women Over 30 Are Better
2418 N 9 Months in Sac
2419 N Cucumbers Are Better
2421 N Honeymoon Guide
2422 N Eat Yourself Healthy
2423 N Sex After 40?
2424 N Sex After 50?
2425 N Women Over 40 Are Better
2426 N Women Over 50 Are Better
2427 N Over The Hill
2428 N Beer Is Better
2429 N Married to a Computer
2430 N Sex After 30?
2431 N Happy B'day Old Fart
2432 N Big Weenies

2433 N Games Play With Pussy
2434 N Sex And Marriage
2435 N Baby's First Year
2436 N How To Love A New Yorker
2437 N The Retirement Book
2438 N Dog Farts
2439 N Handling His Mid-Life Crisis
2440 N How To Love A Texan
2441 N Bedtime Stories...Kitty
2442 N Bedtime Stories...Doggie
2443 N 60 With Sizzle!
2444 N The Wedding Night
2445 N Woman's Birthday Wish
2446 N The PMS Book
2447 N The Pregnant Father
2448 N Games Play In Bed
2449 N The Barf Book
2450 N How To Pick Up Girls
2451 N How To Pick Up Guys
2452 N Driving Amongst Idiots
2453 N Beginner's Sex Manual
2454 N Get Well
2455 N Unspeakably Rotten Cartoons
2456 N For A Million Bucks...
2457 N Hooters
2458 N Adult Connect the Dots
2459 N Once Upon A Mattress
2460 N Golfing Amongst Idiots
2461 N Marry Me, Marry Me
2462 N Smokers Are People, Too

FUN BOOKS $3.00

2026 Games Play In Bed
2034 You're Over 40 When...
2042 Cucumbers Are Better
2064 Wedding Night
2067 It's Time To Retire When...
2068 Sex Manual...Over 30
2102 You're Over 50 When...
2127 Your Golf Game
2131 The Fart Book
2136 The Shit List
2148 Dear Teacher
2166 Survived Catholic School
2177 You're Over The Hill
2180 Italian Sex Manual
2181 Jewish Sex Manual
2192 You're Over 30 When...
2195 Beer Is Better
2203 The Last Fart Book
2205 Sex After 40?
2210 Sex After Marriage?
2213 Women Over 50 Are Better
2217 Sex After 50?
2224 Life's A Picnic...Big Weenie
2225 Women Over 40 Are Better
2226 C.R.S.
2227 Happy Birthday/Year Older
2229 You're A Redneck
2233 Small Busted Women
2234 You're Over 60
2235 You Know You're Over 70

2236 Nose Picker's Guide
2237 55 & Picking Up Speed
2240 Dumb Men Jokes
2241 Cats Are Better Than Men
2242 Working Woman's Doodle
2243 Working Man's Doodle
2244 Words of Wisdom
2245 Potty Potpourri

HARDCOVER BOOKS $8.95

2350 Sailing
2351 Computers
2352 Cats
2353 Tennis
2354 Bowling
2355 Parenting
2356 Fitness
2357 Golf
2358 Fishing
2359 Bathrooms
2360 Biking
2361 Running
2362 Skiing
2363 Doctors
2364 Lawyers
2365 Teachers
2366 Nurses
2367 Firefighters
2368 Marines

Ivory Tower Publishing Co., Inc., 125 Walnut St., P.O. Box 9132, Watertown, MA 02272-9132   Tel: (617) 923-1111